EVERYDAY ECONO

BUDGETING

Blaine Wiseman

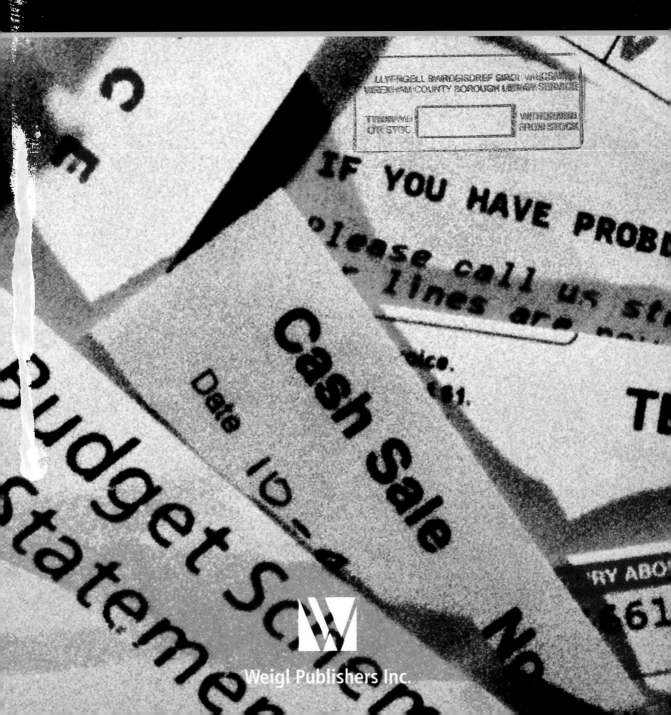

Weigl Publishers Inc.

Published by Weigl Publishers Inc.
350 5th Avenue, Suite 3304, PMB 6G
New York, NY 10118-0069

Website: www.weigl.com

Library of Congress Cataloging-in-Publication Data available upon request.
Fax 1-866-44-WEIGL for the attention of the Publishing Records department.

ISBN 978-1-60596-643-4 (hard cover)
ISBN 978-1-60596-644-1 (soft cover)

Printed in China
1 2 3 4 5 6 7 8 9 0 13 12 11 10 09

Weigl acknowledges Getty Images as its primary image supplier for this title.

Project Coordinator **Heather C. Hudak** | Designer **Terry Paulhus** | Layout **Kathryn Livingstone**

All of the Internet URLs given in the book were valid at the time of publication. However, due to the dynamic nature of the Internet, some addresses may have changed, or sites may have ceased to exist since publication. While the author and publisher regret any inconvenience this may cause readers, no responsibility for any such changes can be accepted by either the author or the publisher.

CONTENTS

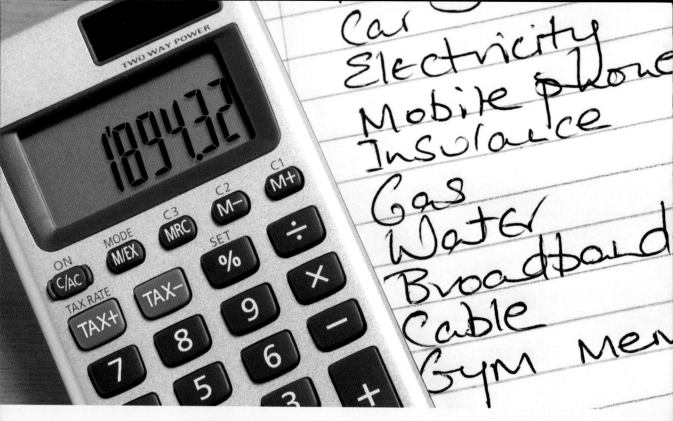

BUDGETING VOCABULARY

EXPENSES products and services that money is spent on
INCOME money received or earned
UTILITIES resources used in a home, such as gas, water, and electricity

What is Budgeting?

Budgeting is the responsible management of a person's money. When people save their money to buy something that they want, this is a basic form of budgeting. Adults may budget their money so they can pay for housing, food, clothing, and other **expenses**. The government has a budget that manages money for roads, schools, hospitals, and other community expenses.

A budget is a plan. Before people can budget, they must know how much money they earn and how much money they spend. Another important part of budgeting is knowing where money comes from and how it is being spent. Once people understand these concepts, they can begin creating a plan for saving and spending money.

101.74
97.31
98.77
19.95
40.00
45.00
...bership
1894.3...

Keeping a record of expenses is part of budgeting.

Money that is earned is called **income**. For many adults, income is acquired through a job. People get paid for doing work. For children, income may come from a part-time job, an allowance, or money earned doing chores.

Expenses are any goods and services that are purchased. Common monthly expenses for adults include **utilities**, such as heat, water, and electricity. Common expenses for children might be books, toys, or games.

By understanding income and expenses, and by planning for the future, a person can balance income and expenses to responsibly manage money.

Budgeting can help people save money and keep track of their expenses.

ELECTED chosen to
represent others
COMMODITIES items that
can be exchanged
FUNDS money reserved for
a particular purpose
INCOME TAX a tax on a
person's annual income
SALARY yearly earnings
of a worker
TAXES fees collected by a
government from its citizens

When Did Budgeting Begin?

Throughout history, budgeting has played an important role in how people manage their money and resources.

10,000–6000 BC People trade cows, grain, and other **commodities**.

3000 BC–525 BC Ancient Egyptian Pharoahs place **taxes** on cooking oil. The tax is used as form of income for Egypt.

27 BC–14 AD Rome's first Emperor, Caesar Augustus, introduces a five percent tax. Income generated by the tax is spent on military retirement **funds**.

10,000-6000 BC | 3000 BC-525 BC | 27 BC-14 AD

1800s In England, the government meets to discuss how to spend the nation's money. The plans are carried in a leather bag, called the "budget." The word comes from the French word *bougette*, which means "purse."

1807 French Emperor Napoleon forms the Cour des Comptes, or Court of Accountants. This is a group of people **elected** to plan the country's budget.

1868–1874 William Gladstone, in charge of England's budget, spends less money on the military and more on public education. He also lowers taxes to help businesses generate more income for the country.

1861 The first **income tax** is issued in the United States. The tax is three percent on any **salary** higher than $800 per year. Today, collecting income tax is a common way for countries to generate income.

1997 President Clinton passes the Balanced Budget Act. The act takes funding from areas such as health care to ensure that the nation's budget is balanced.

1807

1868-1874

1997

BUDGETING VOCABULARY

AMERICAN REVOLUTION
a war that took place between 1775 and 1783 in which American colonists gained independence from Britain

COLONISTS people who settled in the United States

ECONOMIC having to do with the wealth and resources of a country

FINANCIAL having to do with finances or money

Budgeting in the United States

Budgeting is, and always has been, an important aspect of American life. Just like today, early settlers had to budget their money and goods in order to survive during difficult **economic** times.

During the **American Revolution**, for example, Americans felt that they should not have to pay taxes to England. **Colonists** believed their taxes should be used to help the colonies. Many of the budgeting and **financial** decisions made as a result of the American Revolution are still in use today.

In 1928, the Great Depression struck the United States, and many people lost their jobs. By 1933, 15 million U.S. citizens—or one-quarter of the nation's population—were unemployed.

The Great Depression was a time of economic hardship. Many people were unemployed and could not afford basic needs.

During the Depression, budgeting was very important. There was widespread hunger and homelessness because people could not afford food or housing. Managing money responsibly before, during, and after the Depression helped some people cope with the financial crisis.

Today, the government creates a budget every year. This way, the government can plan how it will make and spend the country's money. Creating a responsible, working budget is important for the government and all of the people it represents.

The American Revolution left the newly formed nation with a large debt to repay.

BUDGETING VOCABULARY

MORTGAGES payments for ownership of a property

How do Budgets Work?

Budgets work only as well as they are planned and managed. Budgeting requires organization, attention, goals, and commitment to a plan. The person who creates the budget is the planner and manager of the budget.

Children might prepare a budget to see if they earn enough allowance to pay their expenses and to save for items they want to buy in the future. Imagine a girl receives a $10 allowance each week, and she wants to buy a $200 mountain bike. If she spends $5 on books each week, she has $5 of her allowance to save.

At the end of the month, she will have saved $20. At this rate, it would take ten months to save enough money for the mountain bike. As the budget manager, the girl can make decisions to save more or to spend more. If she decided to stop spending the $5 on books each week, she could save $40 per month and have enough money to buy the bike in five months.

Counting and recording all of the money a person has earned can help save for wanted items.

Types of Budgets

People and organizations at all levels use budgeting to manage their money and avoid financial problems. The four most common types of budget are personal, household, business, and government.

Personal Budgets

A personal budget is what people use to manage their own money. Comparing a weekly allowance to weekly expenses, such as food, clothing, or entertainment such as video games, is an example of a personal budget.

Household Budgets

A household budget is what people use to manage the combined incomes and expenses of an entire household. This type of budget is common among families. People living together may combine their incomes to pay for expenses, such as mortgages, vacations, or vehicles.

Government Budgets

Municipal, state, and federal governments are responsible for budgeting their money. They need to plan how cities, states, and the nation will pay for services.

Business Budgets

Budgeting is an important aspect of running a business. Most businesses create an annual budget, and many review their budgets every three months. In order to create a business budget, planners must account for everything the company buys and sells, the materials it uses, employee salaries, and many other expenses that businesses encounter.

Governments and Budgets

When a government creates a budget, it takes a large staff of **economists** and **officials** to plan and manage it. This organization is called the budget committee. The budget committee must balance money it makes through taxes, trade, and other sources against expenses such as health care, **pensions**, **debt**, **defense**, and education.

The budget committee must prepare for situations that can disrupt the government's income, such as unstable **markets** or changes in the economy. It must also be prepared for unpredictable expenses, such as war or natural disasters.

Governments collect taxes as a form of income in order to pay for roads and other services.

Whether at a municipal, state, or federal level, governments are responsible for budgeting their money. Municipal governments use budgets to manage income, such as property taxes, and services, such as recycling, trash collection, and road repairs.

State governments are responsible for highways, state parks, and state courts, among many other important institutions. The federal budget takes into account the military, health care, federal courts, and other service institutions that affect the country's entire population.

⊞FAQ

How are taxes collected?
Taxes are collected when people earn and spend money. A common form of tax is income tax. This tax is a portion of a person's income that is paid to the government. It is deducted from a person's paycheck. The government charges sales tax on the purchase of goods or services. A percentage of the total cost of the product is added to the purchase. This money is used to pay for services, such as health care and military.

What is the difference between a finance committee and a budget committee?
A finance committee is responsible for taxation and other forms of revenue, or income. The budget committee is responsible for planning how money will be managed throughout the year. The budget helps guide other committees that make decisions about taxes and spending.

Why Should People Budget?

Whether people earn money by mowing their neighbor's lawn, collecting an allowance, or selling **stocks**, responsible budgeting will ensure that they have a plan for their money. Budgeting becomes more challenging as a person gains more responsibilities.

Understanding the difference between items a person needs and items a person wants is an important part of budgeting. Needs are anything a person must have to survive. These include food, shelter, and clothing. Wants are items a person can live without but desires. The more money a person earns, the more he or she can spend on wants or saving for the future.

Investing in the stock exchange is one way to earn money.

Once people start working in a career, they will likely begin to earn more money. However, they may also have more expenses. Housing payments, such as a mortgage or **rent**, utilities, as well as groceries and entertainment are common expenses for most adults. School **tuition**, fees for playing sports, and debt and credit payments are just a few of the other expenses people may have.

An adult may need a car to get to work. Cars are expensive, and most people cannot afford to buy one without **financing** or taking out a **loan**. Monthly payments are made to the bank or company that provided the loan. As part of owning a car, a person must also pay for fuel, **insurance**, **maintenance**, and repairs.

By learning to budget money at an early age, a person can prepare for the expenses and responsibilities that come later in life.

Budgeting skills can also lead to many careers. Some of the most important positions in politics and business, such as accountants and budget analysts, involve maintaining budgets for governments or companies.

Behind the Scenes

In order to create a successful budget, a person's income must be able to pay all of his or her expenses. The goal of any budget should be to save money. If some money is left over after expenses are paid, this money can be saved for the future. This way, if there are unexpected expenses in the future, there will be money saved to pay for these items. Saved money also can be used to pay for "wants," such as vacations and jewelry.

When people cannot make all of their payments, they need to find ways to adjust their budget. A second job will create more income. Riding a bike instead of driving a car can save a large amount of money every month. Cutting out entertainment or eating cheaper food also can save money.

Using a Budget

Budgets can be done daily, weekly, monthly, or yearly. This budget shows an annual plan. All of the person's income and expenses have been filled in for January. The amount remaining can be put into a savings account for future use. Make a similar chart in your notebook, and try filling in the months based on what you think your expenses and income will be for the year.

	Jan	Feb	Mar	Apr	May	Jun	Jul	Aug	Sep	Oct	Nov	Dec
INCOME												
Babysitting	$20											
Paper Route	$50											
Allowance	$40											
Gifts	$25											
Total	$115											
EXPENSES												
Clothes	$20											
Bus Pass	$10											
Snacks	$10											
Movies	$8											
Shoes	$0											
Gifts	$20											
Books	$5											
MP3s	$3											
Unexpected	$0											
Total	$76											
SAVING												
Remaining	$29											

BUDGETING
VOCABULARY

DEPOSIT money placed in the bank
DISPOSABLE money used to buy wanted items
INTEREST money added to an account at regular intervals

Committing to a Budget

Television commercials encourage people to spend money on toys, video games, clothes, food, and other items. With all of these temptations, it can be a challenge to commit to a budget. There are some tips people can follow to help them maintain a budget and potentially save money.

Savings accounts are a type of bank account designed for saving money. When people **deposit** money into a savings account, it collects **interest**. This makes the money grow. Depositing part of an allowance, birthday money, and other forms of income into a savings account will provide money to buy wanted items in the future.

Money can be saved by keeping spare change in jars labeled with types of expenses.

A handful of coins may not seem like much money, but if the coins are collected over time in a jar, they will add up to a significant sum. Labeling several glass jars with terms such as long-term savings, short-term savings, and **disposable** is one way to budget for different types of expenses. Money can be placed in each jar to help pay for wants and needs.

Long-term expenses include items a person wants to buy in the future, such as a car or college tuition. It may take years to save enough money for these things. Setting a goal to save a specific amount of money by a certain date can help people save money for long-term goals. Money from the long-term savings jar should not be used until the goal has been reached.

Since there is a long time to save for this goal, a small portion of money can be put in this jar.

Money in the short-term savings jar can be used to pay for less-costly items that a person wants to buy soon. This might include an MP3 player or a cell phone.

The jar labeled disposable can be used to buy wanted items right away. This may include movie tickets, shoes, or treats.

Dividing money by purpose will help show how budgeting and responsible money management can help people reach their long- and short-term goals.

Responsible Spending

Spending is a big part of budgeting. It is just as important to monitor spending as it is to watch savings grow.

Committing to a budget is made easier by making responsible spending decisions. This means knowing what to spend money on, why money is being spent, and how to get the best value for each dollar spent.

Some people keep a list of the things they buy and how much these items cost. They highlight their wants and needs in different colors. Then, they review the list regularly to look for trends in their spending habits. For example, do they often buy items they want rather than need? Do they eat out regularly? Are there any items they can cut from their spending?

Understanding spending habits, researching products before buying, and shopping around can help a person save money.

Understanding personal spending and saving habits is part of responsible budgeting.

Before buying a product, it is useful to determine if it is needed immediately. It is also a good idea to learn something about its actual worth, and to check if there are similar products offered at a better price. Company websites usually have product information. There also may be customer reviews online, showing what other people think about the product. They may be able to recommend another product with a better price or value.

When people make an **impulse buy**, they often spend outside their budget or do not get the best value for their money. Before spending money on a product, it is recommended that people shop around to find the best price. This is done by comparing prices at different stores or online in order to get the best deal and to see if the product is on sale. Some stores sell products that are slightly used but in excellent condition. Used products cost less than new ones.

FAQ

What are coupons?
Coupons are documents that can be traded for a discount on a product or service. Manufacturers may print coupons in flyers or newspapers, or provide them online.

What is meant by the term best value for each dollar spend?
When someone gets the best value for his or her dollar, it means they have bought the highest-quality product available for a certain price. For example, if a pair of name brand track shoes costs the same price as a store brand pair, it is a better value to buy the name brand shoes.

Government Budgets

Government budgets balance public money by spending and saving in certain areas. Every year, the federal government creates a budget. People in all parts of the nation review the federal budget to make sure that the government is spending money in a wise, responsible manner. Some people may be unhappy with the budget, but it usually reflects what is best for the country as a whole.

In order to spend more money in one area, the government must take money from another area or raise taxes. For example, if the government chooses to spend more money on the military, it may cut spending on education. This would make people involved in national defense, such as soldiers, happy because there would be more money for better training, weapons, and resources. However, cutting education spending could mean that some schools have to close.

Federal and State Government Budgets

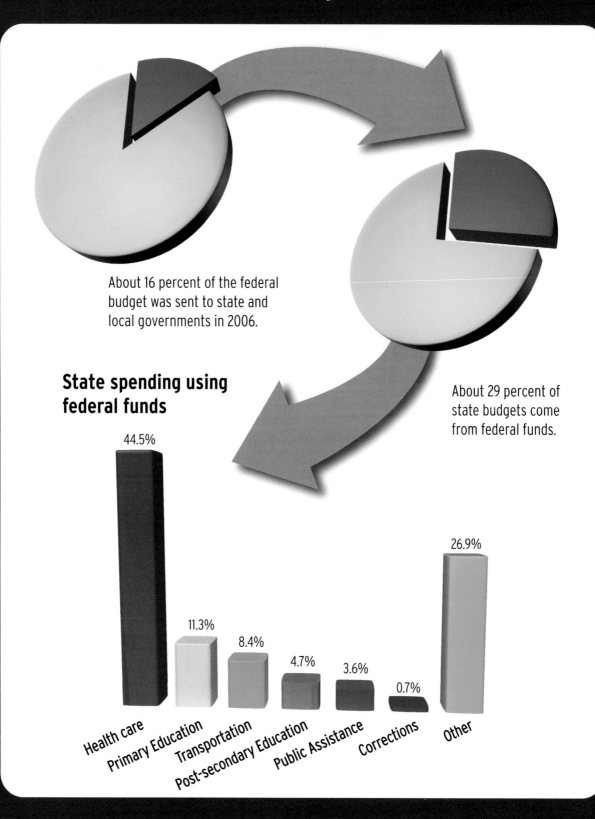

About 16 percent of the federal budget was sent to state and local governments in 2006.

About 29 percent of state budgets come from federal funds.

State spending using federal funds

44.5% Health care

11.3% Primary Education

8.4% Transportation

4.7% Post-secondary Education

3.6% Public Assistance

0.7% Corrections

26.9% Other

Municipal Budgets

Local governments in cities and towns create budgets to decide how best to spend money on community services. Just like a federal budget, a municipal government budget can have a direct impact on a person's life.

Imagine that the local municipal government decides to start a curbside recycling program. This is similar to trash collection, except there is a crew that collects recyclables from a container in front of the house. It would make a community a cleaner place to live, and it would be helping the environment. This program would require recycle bins to be supplied to every home in a community, workers to collect the recycling, trucks to transport the recyclables and the crews, a facility where the recyclables can be sorted, and people to work at this facility. The government would have to pay for these goods and services.

Governments spend money on services such as libraries, trash collection, and playgrounds.

This sort of program could cost millions of dollars, depending on the size of the community. Where would this money come from?

In order to pay for such a program, the government would have to cut spending from other services, such as recreation. The government may spend less money on local sports and playgrounds, for example. People who play baseball would be affected. The government may not be able to pay groundskeepers to take care of the baseball diamonds. Without groundskeepers, the grass would grow long, the fence and backstop might fall over, and there would be no baselines. What would happen to the baseball team if there was no baseball diamond in the community?

Every time a government creates a budget, it is must decide which programs and services need more money and which should get less money or be cut.

⁚FAQ

What is a government surplus?
A surplus happens when a government makes more money than it spends. Governments do not typically try to maintain a surplus, as they want to spend money on providing services to their citizens. However, it also is important that they do not overspend.

What is a government deficit?
A deficit happens when a government spends more money than it has. The government must adjust its budget to avoid overspending. This may result in tax increases or cuts to services.

Budgeting Technology

There are online resources that can be used to plan a budget. Online banking can be used to make transactions from home using a computer. The account **balance** will be updated each time a transaction is made, allowing the user to monitor spending and saving progress. Online banking can be used to transfer funds from one account to another, pay bills, and find new ways to save money.

The Internet offers budgeting programs that can be downloaded. Software includes **spreadsheets**, graphs, tables, and charts that keep track of the budgeting progress. Typing "budget software downloads" into a search engine will display a variety of budget programs.

Budgeting Careers

There are many careers that involve money management. Budget analysts and accountants are people who use budgeting skills to help businesses run effectively.

Budget Analyst

Large companies and organizations rely on budget analysts to manage their finances. Budget analysts develop, analyze, and create budgets and other financial plans. They advise organizations where to spend money, and they predict how much money the organization will earn in the future. The main job of a budget analyst is to help his or her organization make the most money.

Budget analysts usually have a university degree related to finances, such as business or accounting. Budget analysts rely on mathematical and management skills, as well as technical knowledge of spreadsheets and computer programs.

Accountant

Accountants are people who manage money and finances for other people or organizations. They create budgets based on how their client is spending, and based on the goals of the client. As well as planning budgets, accountants deal with sales, taxes, and health care benefits. They also develop new systems for keeping track of their client's money.

The first step to becoming an accountant is to have good math skills. In order to become a certified accountant, a person needs a bachelor degree from a university. Many universities offer accounting degrees, but a business degree is another way to become an accountant. Accountants work at many different levels throughout their careers in order to gain experience.

What Have You Learned?

1 What is budgeting?

2 What is interest?

3 What government organization plans the federal budget?

4 Name four types of budgets.

5 What is an accountant?

6 Name two types of additional payments involved in owning a car.

7 Where does the word "budget" come from?

8 What is impulse buying?

9 What does it mean when a government has a surplus?

10 Name two types of housing payments.

Answers

1. the responsible management of money

2. money added to an account at regular intervals

3. the Budget Committee

4. personal, household, business, and government

5. a person who manages another person's money

6. gas, insurance, repairs, maintenance, and finance or loan payments

7. from the French word *bougette*, which means "purse"

8. buying something without doing research

9. the government collects more money than it spends

10. mortgage and rent

Create Your Own Budget

Budgets are used to help manage money wisely. Use the spreadsheet below to create your own budget. Enter any money that you have earned, already have saved, or are planning to earn. Then, enter all of your regular expenses, as well as any items you would like to purchase. What is the balance? Do you have any money left to save?

Date	Item	Income	Expense	Balance
TOTAL				

Further Research

Many books and websites provide information on budgeting. To learn more about budgeting, borrow books from the library, or surf the Internet.

Most libraries have computers that connect to a database for researching information. If you input a key word, you will be provided with a list of books in the library that contain information on that topic. Non-fiction books are arranged numerically, using their call number. Fiction books are organized alphabetically by the author's last name.

Websites

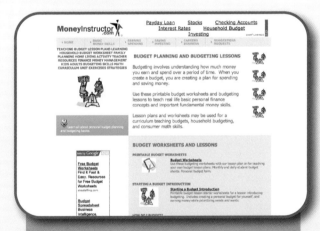

This website has many tips and helpful activities involving budgeting and other financial issues.

www.moneyinstructor.com/ budgeting.asp

For more information about budgeting, check out

www.moneyandstuff.info/pdfs/ SampleBudgetforKids.pdf

Glossary

American Revolution: a war that took place between 1775 and 1783 in which American colonists gained independence from Britain

balance: the amount of money in an account

colonists: people who settled in the United States

commodities: items that can be exchanged

debt: an amount of money that is owed

defense: military organizations that protect the country from attack

deposit: money placed in the bank

disposable: money used to buy wanted items

economic: having to do with the wealth and resources of a country

economists: people who are experts on the economy

elected: chosen to represent others

expenses: anything that money is spent on

financial: having to do with finances, or money

financing: money provided by an auto company or bank, to be paid back, to buy a vehicle or other expensive item

funds: money reserved for a particular purpose

impulse buy: a purchase made without doing research

income: money received or earned

income tax: a tax on a person's annual income

insurance: protection against loss, damage, or theft

interest: money added to an account at regular intervals

loan: money that is borrowed and must be paid back

maintenance: to keep something in good condition

markets: the trade of money and goods on a local or global scale

mortgages: payments for ownership of a property

officials: people who work for a governing body

pensions: regular payments reserved for a person's retirement

rent: a payment made for the use of a property

salary: yearly earnings of a worker

spreadsheets: computer programs or charts used to calculate values

stocks: money raised when a company sell shares, or part ownership

taxes: fees collected by a government from its citizens

tuition: fees to attend a college or university

utilities: resources used in a home, such as gas, water, and electricity

Index